W9-BSA-527

Why Failure
is
Never Final

Turn Setbacks into Steps Forward

GREGORY L. JANTZ, PHD
WITH KEITH WALL

AspirePress

Why Failure Is Never Final:
Turn Setbacks into Steps Forward
Copyright © 2023 Gregory L. Jantz
Published by Aspire Press
An imprint of Tyndale House Ministries
Carol Stream, Illinois
www.hendricksonrose.com

ISBN: 978-1-64938-049-4

The views and opinions expressed in this book are those of the author(s) and do not necessarily express the views of Tyndale House Ministries or Aspire Press, nor is this book intended to be a substitute for mental health treatment or professional counseling. The information in this resource is intended as a guideline for healthy living. Please consult qualified medical, legal, pastoral, and psychological professionals regarding individual concerns.

Tyndale House Ministries and Aspire Press are in no way liable for any context, change of content, or activity for the works listed. Citation of a work does not mean endorsement of all its contents or of other works by the same author.

All Scripture quotations, unless otherwise indicated, are taken from the Holy Bible, New International Version,® NIV.® Copyright ©1973, 1978, 1984, 2011 by Biblica, Inc.® Used by permission of Zondervan. All rights reserved worldwide. www.zondervan.com. The "NIV" and "New International Version" are trademarks registered in the United States Patent and Trademark Office by Biblica, Inc.®

Scripture quotations marked ESV are from The ESV® Bible (The Holy Bible, English Standard Version®), copyright © 2001 by Crossway, a publishing ministry of Good News Publishers. Used by permission. All rights reserved.

Scripture quotations marked NLT are taken from the *Holy Bible*, New Living Translation, copyright ©1996, 2004, 2015 by Tyndale House Foundation. Used by permission of Tyndale House Publishers, Carol Stream, Illinois 60188. All rights reserved.

Printed in the United States of America
010922VP

Contents

Failure Is Not Your Enemy

Failure: It's a topic we're all too familiar with. From the moment we receive our first report card in elementary school, we begin our long, arduous indoctrination into one of the foundational beliefs of Western civilization: Failure is bad—*very* bad.

As children, we learn to fear its many forms—failure to master long division, failure to hit the ball at recess, failure to be the cool one at a school dance, ad infinitum. And kids who get X's in all the wrong columns often wear those marks everywhere, like a permanent tattoo of shame.

In a society like ours, geared to divide the world neatly into winners and losers, failure is unacceptable ... not an option ... a dead end.

As we get older, the stakes grow steadily larger until the consequences of our failures include unfortunate events like unemployment, addiction, bankruptcy, divorce, run-ins with the law, and the seemingly fatal wounding of our sense of self-worth. Over time, we might begin to believe that we *are* failures instead of holding to the realistic perspective that we have only failed at *something in particular*. What a heavy load to drag around!

If all of this sounds depressingly familiar, and you feel like your clothes have suddenly turned to lead, then this is your lucky day. Why? Because you are about to hear some good news for a change. *It doesn't have to be this way. Ever.* The oppressive philosophy that treats failure as cause for shame and self-loathing is, quite frankly, a bunch of baloney.

It is true that failure hurts. It is never anyone's first choice, and it certainly is never pleasant. Failure can make a royal mess of things and overturn all your assumptions about how your life was supposed to turn out. But it is emphatically *not* true that to fail at something—anything—makes you a "failure" or marks the end of your chances of ever succeeding again.

The truth is, if you are alive and willing to venture anything at all, you are going to fail. The question is, How will you think of your failures—and what will you do with them? Will you lie buried under the wreckage for the rest of your life? Or will you light a fire, grab a hammer, and forge something new out of the ruins? Will you see your defeats as mortal blows, or as opportunities to learn and grow stronger?

The idea that failure is actually a priceless gift in disguise is nothing new. Joseph Campbell, author of the classic work *The Hero with a Thousand Faces*, studied the world's ancient stories and discovered that the hero's journey always includes some kind of crushing defeat—even to the point of death. The purpose is to bring the hero face-to-face with their deepest fears. Only then can he or she rise above them, transformed and ready for the next chapter.

IT IS EMPHATICALLY *NOT* TRUE THAT TO FAIL AT SOMETHING—ANYTHING—MAKES YOU A "FAILURE" OR MARKS THE END OF YOUR CHANCES OF EVER SUCCEEDING AGAIN.

The conclusion Campbell drew for us in modern times is simple and succinct: "Where you stumble, there lies your treasure."[1] Authentic treasure is found, it seems, in the very places and circumstances we have been taught to shun.

Carl Jung, the father of analytic psychology, came to the same conclusion. American poet

Robert Bly wrote, "It is said that whenever a friend reported enthusiastically, 'I have just been promoted!' Jung would say, 'I'm very sorry to hear that; but if we all stick together, I think we will get through it.' If a friend arrived depressed and ashamed, saying, 'I've just been fired,' Jung would say, 'Let's open a bottle of wine; this is wonderful news; something good will happen now.'"[2]

A PAINFUL FALL FROM ONE STAGE OF LIFE IS OFTEN PRECISELY THE JOLT WE NEED TO BE PREPARED FOR SOMETHING BETTER.

If you're willing to do the hard work of excavation and reclamation after an avalanche of failure, "something good" can most certainly happen. The treasure waiting in the rubble may take the form of new insight into what's truly important to you, or renewed courage to take fresh risks in pursuit of your dreams.

A painful fall from one stage of life is often precisely the jolt we need to be prepared for something better. Sometimes powerful coincidences rise from the ashes, opening opportunities that could not have existed before the crisis. In all cases we have the potential to emerge as stronger, wiser, and better people for having spent some time in the fire.

Failure can work you over—or work its magic upon you. It's up to you which. If you choose the latter, begin by refusing to see failure as your enemy any longer.

As founder of the mental health clinic The Center: A Place of Hope, I have witnessed countless individuals show up at our doorstep feeling like they have failed miserably, letting down themselves and the people they love. Their failures involve addiction, marital infidelity, financial ruin, legal troubles, or any number of problems caused by poor choices or unfortunate circumstances.

The message my team and I consistently instill in our clients is the same one I want to send to you: Amid your failures, you can always, always, *always* find healing and restoration. You can be refined—not defined—by your failures. You can even become wiser and grow deeper because of your failures.

If you're wondering how such a good outcome could even be possible, stay tuned to learn what God, the one who created you and loves you, has to say about failure. After all, his standards are what define true success and true failure. In the end, his solution for our failures brings lasting redemption.

In the pages ahead, let's walk together on the path toward putting our failures in proper perspective—and growing in God's grace because of them.

"GROW IN THE GRACE AND KNOWLEDGE OF OUR LORD AND SAVIOR JESUS CHRIST. TO HIM BE GLORY BOTH NOW AND FOREVER! AMEN."

—2 Peter 3:18

CHAPTER 1

Your View *of* Failure *and* Why It Matters

The seventeen-year-old aspiring illustrator and cartoonist tried his best.

In 1919 he applied for a job as an office boy at the *Kansas City Star*, a well-respected Midwestern newspaper where Ernest Hemingway had worked as a reporter the year before, but he was rejected for being too old.

Next he was hired as an apprentice at a commercial art shop, but the young illustrator was soon let go after the Christmas rush and found temporary work through the end of the year. Out of a job, he and a partner started their own design business, which led to full-time employment at yet another company, where the pair created animated ads for movie theaters.

Eventually the young man started his own animation company that would go bankrupt within two years.

From there, he decided to move to Hollywood to become a live-action film director.[3] Throughout his long career, his loan and financing requests would be turned down more than three hundred times.[4]

FAILING IN LIFE ISN'T A QUESTION OF *IF* BUT *WHEN*.

The man's name was Walter Elias Disney, but his friends just called him Walt. Despite his early career failures, and being cheated by unscrupulous business partners, Walt and his brother, Roy, kept working and dreaming. It paid off, of course, and Walt Disney Studios was born.

To Be Human Is *to* Fail

Failure is an ugly word we'd rather not think about too much. But failing in life isn't a question of *if* but *when*. It could be failing to make the varsity basketball team, like NBA great Michael Jordan, who ended up excelling on the junior varsity team as a sophomore.

Or perhaps, like science fiction legend Isaac Asimov, it's failing to get into your dream school. After being rejected by medical schools, Asimov was also rejected by Columbia University when he first applied to their graduate chemistry program.

Or even worse, maybe your marriage ended in divorce, you became addicted to drugs or alcohol, you've served jail time, or your business went bankrupt.

The hard truth is that to be human is to fail.

For Walt Disney, failure came in the form of business setbacks and delayed dreams. And we've all heard stories about other famous people who had inauspicious beginnings. Some well-known examples include ...

- **Abraham Lincoln.** Young Abe failed dramatically at many things early in life, including a business partnership that left him deeply in debt, and he lost more than five elections for political office. He even suffered a nervous breakdown after the death of a friend.[5]

- **J. K. Rowling.** Shortly before writing the first book in the Harry Potter series, the now-famous author lost her marriage, became jobless and nearly homeless, and lived off welfare in order to care for her five-month-old daughter.[6]

- **Steve Jobs.** One of the most prolific innovators of our time, Jobs, a college dropout, cofounded Apple Computers but was later fired. Years later, he was reinstated as CEO, leading the launch of products such as the iPod, MacBook, iPad, and iPhone.[7]

- **Theodor Seuss Geisel.** Now known to the world simply as Dr. Seuss (and one of the most beloved children's authors of all time), he was voted "Least Likely to Succeed" by his classmates at Dartmouth College in the 1920s.[8]

- **Vincent Van Gogh.** Saddest of all on this list is Van Gogh, one of the most acclaimed painters of the Post-Impressionist period. After finishing one of his most revered works, *The Starry Night*, he told fellow painter Émile Bernard, "Once again I allowed myself to be led astray into reaching for stars that are too big—another failure—and I have had my fill of that."[9] One year later Van Gogh committed suicide, unaware of how highly the world would eventually value his talents.

Indeed, history has been kind to Van Gogh, but unfortunately, due to a mood disorder, low self-esteem, and persistent financial troubles, Van Gogh never took a high view of himself. In contrast, Abraham Lincoln, who suffered his own major setbacks and struggles, became one of the greatest leaders in US history.

PUT FAILURE IN PERSPECTIVE

Everyone on earth would prefer to succeed rather than fail— 100 percent of the time. But because we are imperfect human beings living in an imperfect world, failure is inevitable. And it happens far more often than we would like.

Some people view failure as it should be: a temporary setback, a lesson learned, a growth opportunity. But for most, failure is viewed more harshly—as a roadblock to future progress, a reason to give up, and evidence they are defective at their core.

A good definition of failure is "when you attempt something and the desired result is less than what you expected." The danger arises when you conclude that you yourself are a "failure"— someone who has a character defect, a lack of talent, or a personality flaw.

Instead, seek to gain a life-affirming attitude toward failure. Rather than viewing it as a catastrophic event, allow it to be a constructive experience ... an ally, not an adversary ... an open door, not an immovable barrier ... a fresh beginning, not a final ending.

Defining What Success Means *to* You

Clearly, Lincoln and Van Gogh perceived and handled failure and success in very different ways. But what about you—how do you personally define failure, and how do you define success? These questions are important, because carving out your own definitions will help to guide and direct your life.

MAKE NO MISTAKE: IT IS NEVER TOO LATE IN LIFE TO REDEFINE YOUR MEANING OF SUCCESS.

Some define success by how many zeros are included in their bank account balance, and some by friendships gained and moments shared with loved ones.

For others, success is based on what people think of them—extrinsic factors such as social media likes, accolades received, or promotions won. In contrast, some define success intrinsically by whether they've achieved a level of joy and peace in their life.

Identifying your own distinct definition is essential, and the earlier in life you can get a handle on it, the more time you will have to achieve it. But make no mistake: It is never too late in life to redefine your meaning of success.

So how do you set out to determine the attributes that will add up to a life of success? Start by asking yourself the following three questions.

1. WHAT DRIVES ME?

First, think about what drives you. Again, is it wealth, fame, prestige, or other outward factors? Or is it intrinsic qualities, such as enjoying harmonious, lasting relationships and having inner peace that is derived from your spiritual belief system? It's safe to say that for most of us, success includes both. But at some point, outward attributes will fail you if you do not also have an intrinsic basis for success.

For example, consider the opening scene of *Citizen Kane*, widely regarded as one of the greatest films ever made. We see the extremely wealthy Charles Foster Kane lying

on his deathbed—old, alone, and miserable. Suddenly he whispers a mysterious name: Rosebud. A childhood sweetheart? A deceased spouse? No (and here's a spoiler alert if you have not seen the film), Rosebud is the name of his childhood sled. It's an heirloom that represents the happiest time of his life, when wealth and success were based on intrinsic elements such as comfort, joy, and contentment.

OUTWARD ATTRIBUTES WILL FAIL YOU IF YOU DO NOT ALSO HAVE AN INTRINSIC BASIS FOR SUCCESS.

When a person's definition of success is based on external factors, there's a good chance he or she will miss out on fulfillment, happiness, contentment, and peace—elements of true success that our Creator intends for us to enjoy.

HOW THE WORLD VIEWS SUCCESS

It's no secret that in most Western nations, the definition of success is contradictory. On one hand, families, schools, and sports teams typically teach that the type of person we are is more important than what we accomplish. On the other hand, the definition thrown at us online and in the media is often the exact opposite: Success is based on money, looks, fame, and power.

It can be toxic and risky to peg our definition of success to extrinsic or material things. We quite literally set ourselves up for failure, because there is always "more" to do, possess, or accomplish, and the goals keep changing.

We do not want to end up like Charles Kane—alone with our material things but bereft of meaningful relationships and internal contentment. It's vital that we make every effort to establish a clear path based on our own aspirations and goals. By creating our own definition of success, we can escape the trap of the culture and age in which we live.

2. WHAT DO I VALUE?

As you endeavor to articulate your definition of success, focus on the things you value most. In order to do that, it's helpful to think with the end in mind. For example, ponder the following questions:

- When your life is drawing to a close, what do you want to have accomplished in terms of extrinsic goals? For example, you invested your time to make the world a better place, worked hard to gain financial stability, accomplished creative pursuits, achieved goals for education, developed your unique talents, and so on.

- What do you hope to have achieved in terms of relationships—work/life balance, a stable marriage, well-adjusted children, close friendships, mentoring legacy, caring for elderly parents?

- What personal dreams do you want to have fulfilled—travel, hobbies, volunteer endeavors, improved wellness and mental health?

- What type of person do you want to be known as? What will people say about you—not at your funeral, in front of others, but afterward, in the privacy of their own homes?

Take the time to make a list of those "end goals" you have in life. Periodically—once or twice a year—review the list and update it as your priorities shift or change.

Defining them will allow you to better hone your definition of both success and failure—because if you have no prevailing or overriding dreams or goals for how you want to live your life, how will you know success—or failure—when you see it? Likewise, how you view failure has everything to do with how you define success.

In this way, as you determine your own definition of success, your goals and aspirations are defined, and you have a clear target in mind.

3. HOW DO OUTSIDE FORCES AFFECT ME?

It's one thing to know that the world has a mixed bag of things to say about success and failure and another to not let them affect you. Most of us would probably say that we don't let peer pressure, the media, and society in general define who we are. But consider the following questions:

- If one of your friends graduated from college debt-free because her parents had paid for her tuition and living expenses, would you resent her?

- If the majority of your friends landed well-paying, full-time jobs with great benefits while you were still stuck in the freelance world, would you feel left out?

- If your roommate is in a serious, committed relationship with an amazing catch, would you feel like there's something wrong with you if you've been single for a long time?

- If a former classmate happened to show up at your high school reunion driving an expensive car, would you feel envious?

- If your best friend had the chance to go on an exciting tour in an exotic foreign country, would you begrudge their opportunity?

These situations may bother you greatly or not bother you in the least. But let's dig a little deeper. What is your gut emotional reaction to the following scenarios?

- You're facing insurmountable financial difficulties and must default on your student loan.

- You suffer an emotional breakdown that causes you to quit your job and enter a treatment facility.

- You have worked as hard as you possibly can and still can't get a decent-paying job.

- Your longtime close friend has suddenly ghosted you, disappearing when you need that person the most.

- Your marriage of twenty years is in trouble, and your spouse has just asked for a divorce.

- Your dream business is failing and you realize you need to declare bankruptcy.

- Your adult child is struggling with drugs, and you need to admit them to rehab.

These are not easy issues to face, and it's only natural to feel sad, depressed, or upset if you've been in any of these situations. But there's a difference between feeling bad about a negative situation and allowing that situation to define you.

Your Failure Template

Let's go back to the comparison we made earlier about Lincoln and Van Gogh. It's impossible to know for sure why Van Gogh succumbed to grief over his failure and Lincoln did not, but one thing is certain: In order to understand how much failures color your life, it's important to look at your "origin story," because looking at the past will inform your present and change your future. When you do this, keep in mind that the point is twofold: (1) to realize whether or not you allow your failures to define you, and (2) to build a clear definition of what success and failure look like for you.

Why does one person see a given failure (being fired, for example) as an insurmountable catastrophe, while another person sees it as a setback that motivates them to try again? Much of how we respond to failure—as well as how we define it—has to do with what we learned early in life. At a young age, our brains develop what we will call a "failure template"—a set of beliefs (whether real or perceived), attitudes, and emotions that form our learned definition of failure and success.

For example, if you were born into a home where social appearances and "looking good" were important, then this value helped form your definition of failure—whether you realize it or not. These early childhood beliefs and the resulting emotions color the way you see the world, well into adulthood. In the above scenario, perhaps the spoken—or unspoken—message you learned was, "Don't let anyone see you sweat" or "If you show weakness, people will eat you alive."

In essence, these messages and attitudes—and the emotions and reactions associated with them—helped form your failure template. The reason they are so powerful is that they reside in the emotional "fight-or-flight" area of your brain, as opposed to the part where you do most of your higher thinking.

OUR FEARS FORM THE ROOTS OF OUR FAILURE TEMPLATES.

One interesting aspect of this "fight-or-flight" area of your brain is that it doesn't relate to a sense of time. For instance, if you were bit by a dog as a young child, you may still be afraid of dogs—even tiny ones. Your "adult self" may tell

you that the three-pound Teacup Chihuahua next door is harmless, but when the little dog growls at you, your heart rate increases and you feel anxious.

The good news is that knowledge is indeed power. In the case of dogs, once you understand why you fear them, you can begin to process those emotions. As you do, you are dealing with that childhood lie that all dogs are vicious and want to bite you. Simply put, you can change your view of dogs by understanding where that "flight" emotion comes from.

So what does all this have to do with failure and how you deal with it? Everything! Because as you understand the origins of your failure template, and what formed it when you were young, you can begin to work through the issues once and for all.

The Relationship *between* Fear *and* Failure

Since our fears form the roots of our failure templates, then it stands to reason that if you can figure out what you're afraid of, you can begin to understand the why. It's critical that you take the time to consider the way you were raised, what you were taught, and how the beliefs and emotions that sprang from these early experiences— your failure template—affects you to this day.

Begin by taking some time to write down at least ten things you are afraid of. Some common examples might include a fear of

- death
- random violence

- disease
- war
- natural disasters
- financial calamity
- never having children
- divorce
- a child struggling with addiction
- the effects of climate change

After you've listed your key fears, identify which of them are rational and which are irrational. Being struck by lightning, for example, might be an irrational fear, since the odds of it happening are extremely low. By unpacking these items, you will begin to understand your earliest core fears and how they continue to shape you.

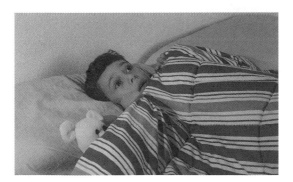

How Do You Define Failure?

Just as it's critical that you form your definition of success, you also need to consider your definition of failure. It may seem like a strange thing to do, but it's worth taking the time and effort to clarify. For some, their definition of failure may be anything less than their definition of success. For example,

- If success means having thirty thousand dollars in your bank account, then failure is having less than that.

- If success means having no debt, then carrying a credit card balance month after month is seen as failure.

- If success means having a college degree, then not achieving that goal is interpreted as failure.

- If success means winning awards, then not receiving any causes you to feel like a failure.

- If success means living in the most expensive house on the block, then failure is owning the cheapest home on the street.

- If success means marrying the best-looking person at your school, then failure is marrying anyone else.

We may scoff and call these definitions ridiculous—but if we are honest with ourselves, we may find a kernel of truth in one or more of these simplistic pairings.

Now consider the fears you identified above, and what we discussed about your "fight-or-flight" lies. Do you see a pattern taking shape—a connection between emotions and experiences from your early childhood, and what constitutes your fears?

As you identify your fears, you will be able to identify what failure has meant for you up to this point in your life. Then and only then can you choose to change your definitions of failure and success. To help you formulate your own balanced definition of failure, consider these words from some well-known successful people:

FAILING IS NOT FATAL. THE WILLINGNESS TO GET UP AND KEEP TRYING IS THE KEY THAT UNLOCKS YOUR ABILITY TO TURN FAILURE INTO SUCCESS.

> *"Failure is merely feedback that there is something blocking the path of the emergence and expansion of the greatest version of yourself."*
> —Attributed to Mother Teresa

"You will make all kinds of mistakes; but as long as you are generous and true, and also fierce, you cannot hurt the world or even seriously distress her."[10]
—Winston Churchill

"My great concern is not whether you have failed, but whether you are content with your failure."
—Attributed to Abraham Lincoln

In the three definitions above, failure is only crippling when we …

- Neglect to gain wisdom from the experience and learn how to do better next time.

- Expect that we won't experience setbacks as a natural part of life.

- Choose to settle rather than be motivated because of setbacks.

No matter how you define failure—and we all have slightly different definitions—the important thing to focus on is that failing is not fatal. The willingness to get up and keep trying is the key that unlocks your ability to turn failure into success.

THE MEANING OF SUCCESS AND FAILURE

Often our perspective of what it means to be a "success" or a "failure" is shaped by the family we grew up in, the social circles we participate in, and the societal messages that influence us. Therefore it is essential to identify for yourself what it means to achieve success or experience failure. Take some time today to reflect on and respond to these pertinent questions:

- In this season of life, what does success mean to you?

- What would you consider a personal "failure" at this point?

- How has your perception of success changed over the years?

- Who in your life do you consider to be successful? How did you come to this conclusion?

| What God Says *about* Failure

The Bible is full of men and women who failed in some way and moved on, with God's grace and power. For now, let's consider two of them.

The Apostle Peter

Think about the apostle Peter, who made his living as a fisherman before Jesus came on the scene. When Jesus first meets him, Peter has been out all night and hasn't caught a thing (Luke 5:1–5). This isn't exactly the definition of career success.

Fast-forward three years to the time just before Jesus' crucifixion. Jesus is eating dinner with the disciples and says to Peter, "This very night, before the rooster crows, you will disown me three times" (Matthew 26:34). Peter protests, but sure enough, he does just that—three times he denies knowing Jesus.

But despite Peter's failure to have Jesus' back in his darkest hour, Peter stayed the course. He did not slink off or disappear from the scene. In fact, even knowing ahead of time that Peter would betray him, Jesus said of Peter, "On this rock I will build my church, and the gates of Hades will not overcome it" (Matthew 16:18).

King David

King David is another biblical figure who failed greatly. He compromised his close fellowship with God and jeopardized his position as king when he committed adultery with another man's wife, then sent the man to the front lines of battle to certain death.

Whether your definition of success is based on internal or external qualities, it's safe to say that King David checked off a lot of failure boxes, and his family suffered terribly as a result of David's actions. Still, God forgave David when he repented of his mistakes and turned his life around. And God was faithful to keep his covenant with him by ensuring that the ancestral line of Jesus came through King David.

EVEN WHEN YOU FAIL, GOD'S LOVE DOES NOT. IF WE CANNOT LOSE HIS LOVE AND HE NEVER GIVES UP ON US, HOW CAN ANY FAILURE CAUSE US TO GIVE UP ON OURSELVES?

No matter how you define success and failure, keep in mind that God's definition has much more to do with *who you are* as his adopted child than with *what you do*. Consider these assurances from God's Word:

You are a chosen people, a royal priesthood, a holy nation, God's special possession, that you may declare the praises of him who called you out of darkness into his wonderful light. Once you were not a people, but now you are the people of God; once you had not received mercy, but now you have received mercy.
1 Peter 2:9–10

As high as the heavens are above the earth,
so great is his love for those who fear him;
as far as the east is from the west,
so far has he removed our transgressions from us.
Psalm 103:11–12

Even when you fail, God's love does not. Even when you doubt yourself, he does not. Because God loves you unconditionally, his love does not waver when you walk in your worst definition of "failure." In fact, "We love because he first loved us" (1 John 4:19).

If we cannot lose his love and he never gives up on us, how can any failure cause us to give up on ourselves? We have a heavenly Father who casts our transgressions "as far as the east is from the west" (Psalm 103:12). And by anyone's definition, that indeed adds up to success.

A final word about that young cartoonist named Walt, who failed to land the job he applied for at the *Kansas City Star*. In 1996, the Walt Disney Company merged with Capital Cities/ABC, whose holdings included the *Kansas City Star*. Yes, the newspaper that didn't want to hire Walt Disney was bought by his company seventy-seven years later.

Never give up—even when people tell you that you lack what it takes. Walt didn't. Honest Abe didn't. And neither should you.

"THAT IS WHY I TELL YOU NOT TO WORRY ABOUT EVERYDAY LIFE—WHETHER YOU HAVE ENOUGH FOOD AND DRINK, OR ENOUGH CLOTHES TO WEAR. ISN'T LIFE MORE THAN FOOD, AND YOUR BODY MORE THAN CLOTHING? LOOK AT THE BIRDS. THEY DON'T PLANT OR HARVEST OR STORE FOOD IN BARNS, FOR YOUR HEAVENLY FATHER FEEDS THEM. AND AREN'T YOU FAR MORE VALUABLE TO HIM THAN THEY ARE? CAN ALL YOUR WORRIES ADD A SINGLE MOMENT TO YOUR LIFE?"

—Matthew 6:25-27 NLT

CHAPTER 2

How Misinterpreting Failure Can Keep You Stuck

Jessie knew the challenge ahead of him would not be easy—he had big shoes to fill and high expectations to meet.

His father, Marco, had owned and operated an auto-repair shop—Marco's Motors—for more than thirty years. Marco grew the business from a tiny garage behind his house, with one mechanic (himself), into a thriving full-service shop with state-of-the-art equipment and many skilled technicians. Along the way, Marco built a loyal clientele, and the shop gained a reputation as a top-notch place to take your car for any need.

Finally, at age sixty-seven, Marco figured he had endured enough work-related backaches and headaches for one lifetime. It was time to hand the business over to his son,

Jessie, and enjoy the fruits of his labor. He had earned the privilege of having more free time to play golf and take vacations with his wife.

Jessie had worked off and on at the shop for years, and now it was his time to step up and lead the team—and take the business into the future. When Jessie took over, however, problems quickly began to surface. While highly skilled at auto repair, Jessie lacked his father's natural people skills, which caused minor issues to become major ones. Also apparent was Jessie's lack of skill at handling the daily tasks that make a business run efficiently—managing inventory, tax planning, responding to customer complaints, and reviewing insurance policies.

Business dropped significantly, along with revenues. Within two years under Jessie's management, Marco's Motors had gone from a thriving business and beloved part of the community to a place to avoid. Jessie got tired of hearing people say, "This place isn't like it used to be," or worse, "You sure don't run things like your dad did." But with customers dwindling and employees quitting, Jessie had to tell his father the truth: He had taken this well-oiled machine and driven it off a cliff.

Marco came out of retirement to try to save the business he had spent decades nurturing. And frankly, he was shocked at the mess he reinherited. As for Jessie, he continued working at the shop as his dad struggled to jump-start it back to life. But he felt ashamed every day as he pulled on his work clothes and grabbed his tools. He had let down his dad, his mom, his employees, his customers—and himself.

After a few months of feeling lousy about himself, he told his dad he was leaving the business to try to find success somewhere else, in another line of work. "I just wanted to get out of there," Jessie recalled later. "I couldn't stay in a place that reminded me every day of how badly I'd blown it."

Jessie thought he might go back to college, which he had tried years earlier before deciding to drop out since he lacked a clear sense of direction. He also considered joining his friend's lawn-care service, or learning a new trade, like plumbing or electrical work.

What he ended up doing, however, was bouncing around from one odd job to another, never finding a landing place where he could start fresh with a chance to thrive. Worse yet, he began to drink heavily to subdue his feelings of shame and soothe his sense of boredom.

Jessie would eventually find his way back to stability a few years later, working as a mechanic at a high-end custom-repair shop. Around the same time, Marco sold his business and returned to retirement.

"It took me many years and more failures to move beyond that experience with Marco's Motors," Jessie explained. "But eventually I figured out who I am and the type of environment I needed to succeed."

Misinterpreting Failure Creates Obstacles

A theme we've touched on previously is worth reiterating here: A sense of failure can either stop us in our tracks or propel us forward toward greater achievement and fulfillment in the future. Jessie made the all-too-common mistake of misinterpreting failure. Sure, he made big mistakes that had disappointing consequences. But no matter the failure he experienced, that didn't mean he was a failure as a person. It didn't mean his future was destined to be a series of failures.

Most of us have done the same thing in different ways. When we fail at something, or *perceive* that we've failed, it may hurt or embarrass us to the point that we shrivel into a self-protective shell. We want to run away and escape the painful situation.

Unfortunately, misinterpreting or "catastrophizing" failure can paralyze us by eroding our inner confidence and making us afraid to try again. Like Jessie, we may fall into the trap of negative thinking that leads us to conclude, "I'm not going to put myself through that again," or even to believe the extreme lie that "I failed; thus I am a failure."

Such self-imposed obstacles can prevent you from achieving your goals and dreams. So in our journey to learn from and overcome feelings of failure, I want to point out how an unhealthy view of failure can thwart your progress and, both figuratively and literally, keep you stuck. If you're aware of these tendencies, you'll be less likely to let them hinder you.

WHEN WE FAIL AT SOMETHING, OR *PERCEIVE* THAT WE'VE FAILED, IT MAY HURT OR EMBARRASS US TO THE POINT THAT WE SHRIVEL INTO A SELF-PROTECTIVE SHELL.

In that spirit, let's look at eight ways failure might be creating obstacles in your life—so that you can clear them out of the way and move ahead freely and confidently.

1. FAILURE CAN LEAD YOU TO QUIT

In the wake of failure, some of the negative messages you've grown up with can activate and hound you into thinking the worst. Perhaps a flustered parent commented, "Why can't you be more like your brother?" Or a shortsighted teacher or coach said something equivalent to "You'll never amount to much." In the face of failure, any such messaging from your past may resurface to convince you that you somehow don't measure up, and probably never will.

Amid actual or perceived failure, the path of least resistance often looks far more attractive than a path of heavier resistance. Jessie made the mistake of giving in to the temptation to quit and walk away, rather than learning from his mistakes and seeking help to make up for his shortcomings.

Granted, it's much easier to give up than to get up, dust ourselves off, and try again. Yet professional and Olympic sports are replete with top athletes who failed more than once on their paths to greatness, and/or had once been told that their chosen sport was not for them.

Fortunately, they refused to listen to the lie. They refused to let moments of failure or discouraging words convince them that they *were* failures. As legendary football coach Vince Lombardi said, "It's not whether you get knocked down; it's whether you get up."[11] These brilliant athletes were knocked down at least once, but they renewed their commitment, jumped back up, and tried again—harder and better.

After Great Britain had withstood the initial devastating onslaught of Nazi forces, Prime Minister Winston Churchill told his fellow citizens, "Never give in, never give in, never, never, never, never—in nothing, great or small, large or petty—never give in except to convictions of honour and good sense."[12] Those words helped rally his besieged nation to continue to stand strong, and eventually Great Britain and its allies prevailed against the Nazi war machine.

"Our greatest weakness lies in giving up," said Thomas Edison. "The most certain way to succeed is always to try just one more time."[13] After many failed projects, Edison's eventual success with the light bulb and other inventions are solid testaments to this principle.

Don't let a failure lead you to quit. Instead, learn from it. Use its lessons to spur you on to new beginnings.

EIGHT WAYS TO GET UP WHEN LIFE KNOCKS YOU DOWN

Everyone has times when they feel knocked down by disappointments and failures. It can be tough to get up and keep fighting. An essential quality—resilience—is what determines who will thrive and who won't. Here are eight strategies to help you brush yourself off and move forward.

1. **Realize you're not alone.** Since everyone on earth encounters adversity of various kinds, many people can relate to your particular struggles.

2. **Don't generalize.** When hit with hard news (a job loss, a breakup, harm caused to others by your actions), it can seem that *everything* in your life has soured. Stay focused on the many good things happening for you.

3. **Draw upon past successes.** Review your history and gain courage from the times you have performed well or overcome hardships.

4. **Write it out.** Expressing your thoughts and feelings in a journal will help you process them and gain clarity.

5. **Practice self-compassion.** Treat yourself with plenty of kindness and grace.

6. **Ask for help.** Seek the support of friends and family members who care about you.

7. **Reframe your perspective.** Realize that adversity often leads to growth opportunities and new pathways.

8. **Look for lessons.** Use hard times to gain insights that will equip you to flourish in the future.

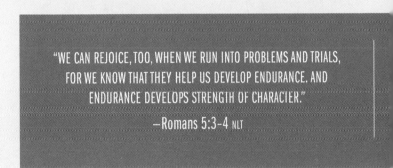

"WE CAN REJOICE, TOO, WHEN WE RUN INTO PROBLEMS AND TRIALS, FOR WE KNOW THAT THEY HELP US DEVELOP ENDURANCE. AND ENDURANCE DEVELOPS STRENGTH OF CHARACTER."

—Romans 5:3-4 NLT

2. FAILURE CAN LEAD YOU TO BLAME OTHERS

No one wants to look stupid, and no one wants to be identified with a failure. So pointing fingers at others can be a convenient "out"—it hurts much less than risking your reputation for being savvy and successful.

But the truth is, tossing others under the bus can be harder on your reputation than it is on those you attempt to blame. Most observers are usually shrewd enough to notice when someone desperately tries to shift blame to others. And think about it: There's really no quicker way to lose the respect of those around you.

BY OWNING UP TO FAILURE, WE MAY ALSO GAIN MORE RESPECT FROM OTHERS THAN IF WE'D PERSISTED IN SHIFTING BLAME.

And conversely, there are few quicker ways to *gain* the trust and respect of others than to admit when you fall short and take responsibility for it—even when you're not solely to blame for the situation.

Essayist John Burroughs is attributed with saying, "A man may fail many times, but he isn't a failure until he begins to blame someone else." Even if others are partially to blame for a failure, we need to

46

own what is ours. What faulty assumptions, misreads, or mistakes did we make that contributed to the undesirable result?

It's essential to recognize and acknowledge our own role in a failure so we can learn and grow wiser from the experience. Paradoxically, by owning up to failure, we may also gain more respect from others than if we'd persisted in shifting blame.

3. FAILURE CAN LEAD TO DENIAL AND AVOIDANCE

We all have blind spots—those areas of life in which we lack understanding or impartiality. We avoid addressing them because it's uncomfortable to take a close, honest look. Blind spots can keep us from acknowledging the hard truth of our failures—that we have shortcomings and have perhaps used poor judgment.

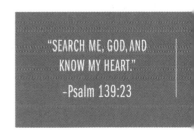

"SEARCH ME, GOD, AND KNOW MY HEART."
-Psalm 139:23

Seeking out your blind spots takes deliberate courage and effort. Consider asking trusted friends, family members, or colleagues for feedback on what they perceive as your areas of denial and avoidance. Armed with this new self-awareness, you can start to take steps toward corrective action.

As Jessie discovered the hard way, he was brilliant at fixing machines but not so great at managing a business. He lacked natural skills at handling conflict, overseeing details, and addressing problems efficiently. His strengths were overshadowed by his weaknesses.

BLIND SPOTS CAN KEEP US FROM ACKNOWLEDGING THE HARD TRUTH OF OUR FAILURES— THAT WE HAVE SHORTCOMINGS.

Like Jessie, we are all a combination of strengths and weaknesses. We're great at some things and not so great at others. It's vital that we not allow the latter truth to dominate the former one. While it's important to be mindful of our weaknesses and blind spots, the key to bouncing back from failure is to focus on our strengths.

4. FAILURE CAN LEAD TO ANGER AND BITTERNESS

As time passed, Jessie found himself struggling with anger over his failed attempt to take over his father's business. Sometimes he felt mad at himself for agreeing to become the top boss in the first place, and sometimes he blamed others for not stepping in to help him more.

Anger over a failure can be directed toward ourselves, others, our circumstances, or God. It's a natural response to perceived unfairness, and it's part of being human. And anger is a two-edged sword: It can be a negative force that smolders into deeply held bitterness, *or it can* serve as a positive force that fuels us to try again, try harder, and try more wisely in the future. The cliché is so true: Hardship can make you bitter or better. The choice is yours. Ask yourself, *Will I wallow in anger and bitterness, or will I let this failure motivate me to greater and wiser attempts?* This is one aspect of your life that you *can* control.

5. FAILURE CAN LEAD TO SELF-DESTRUCTIVE BEHAVIOR

Regardless of whether a failure just "happens" or we have made a mistake to cause it, failure can bring a sense of shame. And shame is one of the most toxic emotions a person can experience. My dictionary calls it "a painful emotion caused by consciousness of guilt, shortcoming, or impropriety."[14]

THE KEY TO BOUNCING BACK FROM FAILURE IS TO FOCUS ON OUR STRENGTHS.

Feeling bad about ourselves can drive us to anesthetize the pain with activities or substances that are of little help—and often harmful. We may try to self-medicate by bingeing on "comfort"

foods, watching too much TV, overspending, or extensively surfing and shopping online. Deeper states of shame may push us to try numbing the hurt by drinking too much alcohol or misusing antidepressants, opioids, cannabis, or nicotine. All such attempts can only bring greater harm to our minds, bodies, and emotions.

SHAME IS ONE OF THE MOST TOXIC EMOTIONS A PERSON CAN EXPERIENCE.

And this is where failure begets failure. A single setback, addressed with self-destructive escapism, pulls you into a downward spiral of failure upon failure, making recovery far more difficult.

But it doesn't have to be this way. If you find yourself descending into unhealthy behaviors, I strongly recommend that you see a professional counselor immediately. Break that downward spiral now, before it pulls you down any further.

6. FAILURE CAN LEAD TO SELF-PITY AND SELF-BLAME

We are usually our own worst critics. When struggling to get over failure, we often catastrophize the situation, making it out to be much worse than it actually is. We may avoid contact with others, assuming that everyone is smirking at us. And we might also make the unhealthy mistake of indulging in *self-pity* and *self-blame*.

- **Self-pity** convinces us that failure is final and beyond recovery.

- **Self-blame**, or negative self-talk, floods our minds and emotions, shouting that we're morons and that we've blown it big-time.

Sometimes the combination degenerates into depression, which brings devastating feelings of worthlessness and hopelessness. We'd rather just curl up and sleep it all away.

Author R. G. Ingersoll made an astute observation when he wrote, "The greatest test of courage on earth is to bear defeat without losing heart."[15] In other words, in the face of failure or defeat, we will be much healthier and happier, and recover from our blunders much more quickly, if we refuse to stoop to self-pity and self-blame. In modern-day language, we should "get over ourselves," dust ourselves off, confess our failure, ask forgiveness of anyone we may have offended, and get on with life.

Instead of losing heart, lose the self-loathing. Refuse to listen to the scathing self-talk. Truth is, no one else cares about your failure, or perceived failure, as much as you think. And truth is, failure is only final if you give up.

7. FAILURE CAN LEAD TO DOUBTING YOURSELF

Any kind of failure can rattle us and make us question ourselves. Whether from critical self-talk or disparaging comments from others, chastisement may even cause us to doubt our abilities and struggle with a damaged sense of worth.

In the face of nearly ruining Marco's Motors, Jessie battled feelings of anger and bitterness and the temptation to protect his ego. What's more, he began to doubt he would ever be anything other than a "grease monkey"—a not-so-complimentary term he applied to himself, even though he was highly skilled at his craft.

Some days Jessie engaged in the comparison game, sizing himself up against friends or colleagues who seemed to have achieved more success than he had: *Maybe if I'd stuck it out in college and gotten a degree, I'd be better off. Or maybe if I'd tried a different kind of work, like most of my friends, then I'd have all the things they enjoy. Maybe I'm not as talented as I thought I was.*

FAILURE IS ONLY FINAL IF YOU GIVE UP.

You can see the damage that occurs when we let negative thoughts run rampant in the face of failure. Bitterness, shame, self-pity, and self-blame clear the path to self-doubt and a devalued sense of worth—making recovery even tougher. When you doubt your abilities and self-worth, it's essential to remember that God has given you irrevocable gifts (Romans 11:29), and your value is not dependent on successes or failures but on your identity as God's child:

When the kindness and love of God our Savior appeared, he saved us, not because of righteous things we had done, but because of his mercy. He saved us through the washing of rebirth and renewal by the Holy Spirit, whom he poured out on us generously through Jesus Christ our Savior, so that, having been justified by his grace, we might become heirs having the hope of eternal life.

Titus 3:4–7

BUILD YOUR SELF-CONFIDENCE

A sense of failure naturally brings up feelings of self-doubt. To bolster your self-confidence as you move forward to try again, remember what the Lord told Joshua: "Have I not commanded you? Be strong and courageous. Do not be afraid; do not be discouraged, for the LORD your God will be with you wherever you go" (Joshua 1:9). Also consider these strategies:

- **Stop ruminating on past mistakes.** Make a list of things you can do to disrupt negative thoughts the next time you want to beat yourself up over blunders. For example, meditate on Psalm 103:12, which assures us, "As far as the east is from the west, so far has he removed our transgressions from us." Also, connect with a grace-giving friend who will affirm that you are accepted as you are.

- **Don't believe everything you think.** Identify the messages that run through your mind, nurturing the positive ones and dispelling the negative ones.

- **Create a healthy environment.** Surround yourself with those who value and appreciate your qualities. Find people who will always tell you the truth, with love and grace.

- **Love others.** Set a daily goal of making a positive difference in the life of someone you know or meet. Studies show that when people are kind to others, it increases their own self-esteem and overall happiness.

- **Identify one issue and work through it.** All of us have weaknesses or shortcomings that hold us back. Think about one aspect you want to improve upon and get help from books, podcasts, a counselor, or close friends.

- **Engage with life in ways that leave you feeling empowered.** For example, spend less time on your phone and more time pursuing activities that are life-giving to you.

"HAVE I NOT COMMANDED YOU? BE STRONG AND COURAGEOUS. DO NOT BE AFRAID; DO NOT BE DISCOURAGED, FOR THE LORD YOUR GOD WILL BE WITH YOU WHEREVER YOU GO."

-Joshua 1:9

8. FAILURE CAN LEAD TO QUESTIONING GOD

After a failure, even those of us who profess faith in a loving God may question why he didn't step in and help us. After all, doesn't he want us to succeed in all we do? Doesn't he want us to avoid embarrassment and hardship when things don't go as we'd hoped?

GOD IS INDEED LOVING AND CARES DEEPLY AND PERSONALLY ABOUT US. HE WANTS WHAT'S *BEST* FOR US.

Because we live one day at a time— one moment at a time—we can't foresee how our mistakes fit into the big-picture plans God has for our lives. We can't specifically envision how today's failure will shape us and equip us for tomorrow's fruitfulness.

Yet we know for certain from Scripture that God is indeed loving and that he cares deeply and personally about us. We can draw courage and comfort from the words of Jeremiah 29:11: "'I know the plans I have for you,' declares the LORD, 'plans to prosper you and not to harm you, plans to give you hope and a future.'"

We also must recognize that God's plans to give us a hope and future don't always unfold the way we want them to. He wants what's *best* for us, and his best may or may not be what we've prayed and hoped for.

For this reason, the Bible does not promise that we'll get everything we ask for. He knows what we need infinitely better than we do, and he allows us to go through tough times—yes, even failures and perceived failures—in order to help us grow in wisdom, perseverance, and character. As Scripture assures us, "In all things God works for the good of those who love him, who have been called according to his purpose" (Romans 8:28).

You may wonder whether God has abandoned you amid failure. Rest assured that he has not. When you trust in him, "he will never leave you nor forsake you" (Deuteronomy 31:6). He's there for you and will guide you through the process of making things right. It may even hurt a bit, but he's allowed the pain in order to make you a stronger, better, wiser person.

■ ■ ■

In this chapter, we've looked at several ways in which failure, if not addressed, can drag us down and keep us stuck. If we're not careful, any of them can cause us to stumble into the pit of despair.

But if we refuse to dwell on our failures and instead take constructive action, we can head off such complications before they have a chance to pull us down. The next chapter will show us how.

"[GOD] SAID TO ME, 'MY GRACE IS SUFFICIENT FOR YOU, FOR MY POWER IS MADE PERFECT IN WEAKNESS.' THEREFORE I WILL BOAST ALL THE MORE GLADLY ABOUT MY WEAKNESSES, SO THAT CHRIST'S POWER MAY REST ON ME. THAT IS WHY, FOR CHRIST'S SAKE, I DELIGHT IN WEAKNESSES, IN INSULTS, IN HARDSHIPS, IN PERSECUTIONS, IN DIFFICULTIES. FOR WHEN I AM WEAK, THEN I AM STRONG."

—2 Corinthians 12:9-10

SO YOU'VE HAD A SETBACK?

Interpreting Failure through God's Eyes

❏ **When I'm tempted to quit ...**

I will commit to learn from the experience and allow its lessons to spur me on to new beginnings.

"I can do all things through him who gives me strength." (Phil. 4:13)

❏ **When I want to blame someone else ...**

I will take responsibility for my own part in the failure.

"Whoever conceals their sins does not prosper, but the one who confesses and renounces them finds mercy." (Prov. 28:13)

❏ **When I want to live in denial and avoidance ...**

I will seek out my blind spots by asking trusted friends, family members, or colleagues for feedback.

"We all stumble in many ways. Anyone who is never at fault in what they say is perfect, able to keep their whole body in check." (James 3:2)

❏ **When I'm faced with the choice to be angry or bitter ...**

I will choose "better" over "bitter" and allow my setback to motivate me to greater and wiser attempts.

"Get rid of all bitterness, rage and anger, brawling and slander, along with every form of malice." (Eph. 4:31)

❏ **When I struggle with self-destructive behavior ...**

I will seek professional counseling to help stop the downward spiral.

"Victory is won through many advisers." (Prov. 11:14)

❏ **When I want to wallow in self-pity or self-blame ...**

I will dust myself off, confess my failure, ask forgiveness of anyone I may have offended, and get on with my life.

"If we confess our sins, he is faithful and just and will forgive us our sins and purify us from all unrighteousness." (1 John 1:9)

❑ When I doubt myself ...

I will remember that God has given me irrevocable gifts, and that my value is not dependent on successes or failures but on my identity as God's child.

"We have different gifts, according to the grace given to each of us." (Rom. 12:6)

"God shows his love for us in that while we were still sinners, Christ died for us." (Rom. 5:8)

❑ When I question God ...

I will trust that he cares deeply and wants the best for me, and that he is working even my failures together for good.

"We do not lose heart.... For our light and momentary troubles are achieving for us an eternal glory that far outweighs them all." (2 Cor. 4:16–17)

CHAPTER 3

Reframing Your View *of* Failure

Chantel sat across from me in my counseling office with every appearance of being an accomplished and successful person, wearing a tailored suit and designer glasses, an expensive handbag and the latest smartphone sitting beside her.

And I soon learned that she was indeed highly accomplished. At age forty-six, she had risen through the ranks of a large software company to become vice president of marketing. Apparently, there was talk of grooming her to become CEO one day.

Chantel traveled around the world almost weekly to meet with other executives in her industry, always staying in the finest hotels and dining at exclusive restaurants.

She also served on the board of directors for two other firms and had won numerous professional awards.

All of this made her impressive and admirable, for sure. There was just one problem: The rest of her life—her personal life—was on the brink of failure. With such a demanding job, Chantel had little time for Marcus, her college sweetheart she'd been married to for twenty-one years. Her adolescent children hardly spoke to her and were getting into serious trouble, including drug use, school suspension, and run-ins with the law. Chantel rarely spent time with her elderly parents who lived nearby and squeezed in only the occasional coffee meet-up with friends.

SUCCESS CAN BE A DOUBLE-EDGED SWORD. WITHOUT BALANCE, A SUCCESSFUL LIFE IN ONE AREA CAN LEAD TO PROBLEMS IN OTHER AREAS.

"I feel like lots of people admire me, but few truly love me or know me," she said. "This is the person I've become—successful but isolated and irrelevant to the people closest to me."

Chantel had come to realize that success can be a double-edged sword. Without balance, a successful life in one area can lead to problems in other areas.

In fact, Marcus had recently mentioned the possibility of divorce and had contacted an attorney. Passing Chantel in the upstairs hallway at home, one of her teenagers remarked, "If you and Dad split up, I'm going to live with him. What would be the point of living with you? You're never around, and you don't care."

That hurt her to the core. And it was another reason for Chantel to take a hard look at her life, beyond her high-flying career achievements. She thought about her parents, whom she hadn't talked to in several weeks, and also her friends—they had stopped reaching out because she was always too busy for them.

"I've failed the people dearest to me," she lamented. "All my life, I've always said that my family and friends are what's most important to me. But now I see that my choices haven't backed up my words."

Chantel paused to collect her thoughts, then continued. "Now it feels like my life is imploding. Except for my job title and bank account—for whatever that matters. I have royally screwed up."

Despite her mistakes and missteps along the way, Chantel was still in a position to make things right. I assured her that failure—of any kind—is never beyond redemption and repair. There is always reason for hope.

Let me share with you fourteen ideas I shared with Chantel that are essential for anyone who seeks to reframe their failures and grow beyond them into a deeper, wiser person.

1. Move Forward, Not Backward

When failure knocks us down, we can choose to move forward or backward. The key word here is *choose*.

Failure is not finality but rather a learning opportunity. If you can apply what you learned, you've transformed a blunder into a blessing, a disadvantage into an advantage.

FAILURE OF ANY KIND IS NEVER BEYOND REDEMPTION AND REPAIR. THERE IS ALWAYS REASON FOR HOPE.

Like most people, I've failed more times than I care to remember. When my wife, LaFon, and I were just starting The Center more than thirty years ago, we made dozens of mistakes involving finances, personnel, payroll practices, office leasing, and on and on.

There were many years when we had serious doubts (probably justified) about our ability to launch and operate a large mental health clinic. But we persevered and pressed on, despite our stumbles, because we felt a sense of mission. We believed God had a purpose for our lives, a call to something meaningful and significant.

I hope you feel the same way. Despite your mistakes, you have a mission to pursue and a path forward.

Because of the way I've come to view failure—as "something that didn't work" versus "I'm worthless"—I've learned from my mistakes and grown because of them. I've made something out of the life experiences that many of us perceive as a waste of time or a loss.

FAILURE IS NOT FINALITY BUT RATHER A LEARNING OPPORTUNITY.

When most people fail, they believe they're in a negative position compared to when they began—or even worse, they believe *they* are not good enough. But if you turn that around and realize the issue isn't failure itself but rather

not learning from the failure, you're more equipped to move ahead and excel, and afterward you'll be richer in life experience.

Thomas Edison, inventor of the first commercially viable light bulb, had once conducted at least nine thousand experiments to develop a storage battery—to no avail. When a colleague remarked with pity that Edison had worked hard but obtained no results, Edison replied, "Results! Why, man, I have gotten a lot of results! I know several thousand things that won't work."[16]

THE GREAT MOMENTS IN HISTORY AND HUMAN INVENTION HAVE COME FROM PEOPLE WHO GREW FROM THEIR FAILURES INSTEAD OF BEING LIMITED BY THEM.

Can you imagine if he had given up? What if he had perceived his failures as confirmation of his own shortcomings or the unworthiness of his goal? Edison took his failures as learning experiences, and they eventually led him to one of the most important inventions of the nineteenth century.

Today, a similar attitude is held by successful researchers, scientists, entrepreneurs, and athletes. These are men and women who allow their life experiences to propel them forward, squeezing the last drop of potential from everything that's happened so that even the failures are positive.

When we hear the stories of great people's lives, we recognize that their failures paved the way to their ultimate success. Failure is part of where they've come from and where they end up going. The great moments in history and human invention have come from people who *grew from their failures instead of being limited by them.*

And we're no different. Inside every person, our Creator has placed a potential for greatness that can be molded and strengthened by failure. In fact, true character is forged in these moments of crisis and failure. The more life challenges you confront with an attitude of learning, the more you will develop as a well-rounded person.

2. Come Clean *about* Your Mistakes

The best way to move past—and learn from—failures is to address them openly and honestly.

Easier said than done, I know. That's because all of us would prefer to avoid painful topics and hide the truth about our troubles—especially the ones we brought on ourselves or on those we love.

But addressing the truth about our mistakes begins the process of finding freedom. I often remind myself and my counseling clients of the Scripture passage that tells us, "You will know the truth, and the truth will set you free" (John 8:32).

Even as a kid, I learned it was liberating to own up to something I'd done that I wasn't proud of. Trying to keep a secret from my parents, a teacher, or a friend was exhausting, like walking around with my pockets full of rocks. The moment I told the truth, it was as if all that weight would disappear. Even if there were still consequences to face, I always felt better.

That's what the concept of confession is all about—setting us free from the dread of discovery when we're in the wrong. Taking responsibility serves as a powerful reminder that we're only human, after all.

Fear of exposure arises, in part, from the misguided belief that we ought to be more than we are, when the fact is that God expects no such thing. The moment we admit our failures and cut ourselves some slack, we find the strength and motivation to make better choices in the future.

3. Forgive Yourself

In times of failure, we tend to heap guilt and shame upon ourselves. As we lie awake in the wee hours of the morning, our own perceived offenses grow in our minds to monstrous proportions. They cease being about what we have done and become the unfortunate evidence of who we are—*horrible human beings*. This is the mindset of people who suffer from a deeply entrenched belief in their own worthlessness.

THE MOMENT WE ADMIT OUR FAILURES AND CUT OURSELVES SOME SLACK, WE FIND THE STRENGTH AND MOTIVATION TO MAKE BETTER CHOICES IN THE FUTURE.

It's not true, of course. Take away the word *horrible*, and you've got the truth of it: We're all just human beings, flawed and prone to all kinds of blunders.

Have you made choices you are not proud of? Certainly.

Have you disappointed others who had a right to depend on you? Yes.

Have you betrayed someone's trust? Taken something that didn't belong to you? Lied to protect yourself from exposure? Exaggerated the truth just because you could? Cheated on an exam or other kind of test? Broken promises to God, yourself, and others? Put someone else in harm's way to gratify yourself?

Most likely you have failed in at least some of these ways, and in many others as well. How do I know? Because you are human, and every human on earth is a combination of strengths and weaknesses, assets and liabilities, successes and failures.

BY FORGIVING YOURSELF, YOU'RE EMPOWERED TO REGAIN YOUR FOOTING AND STEP ONWARD.

The irony is that we typically hold ourselves to a standard that's much higher than what we expect of others. It's actually a reversed kind of arrogance that causes us to set up a wall of shame in our minds, where all our flaws, large and small, are on display under bright lights. Such self-focus distracts from the honor due to God for what he has done for us in forgiving our failures. By forgiving yourself, you're empowered to regain your footing and step onward.

4. Avoid Self-Sabotage

Life is challenging enough without encountering an unexpected complication: Yourself. On the road to achievement, some people put obstacles in their own way, usually without knowing it.

All of us are prone to undermining our best intentions and aspirations, but that doesn't mean we are doomed to repeat unhealthy cycles. Following are some strategies to steer you away from sabotaging your own efforts.

- **Make choices today that will ensure a better tomorrow.** Consistently wise decisions about how you live day by day and moment by moment will take you a giant step closer toward a healthy, satisfying future.

- **Resist the urge to find comfort in food or drink.** This, of course, is one of the most prevalent means of self-sabotage. Substance misuse or abuse— whether of food, alcohol, or drugs—seems helpful at the moment, but it is extremely harmful in the long haul.

- **Push past procrastination.** Procrastination is one of the most common—and easily rationalized— forms of self-sabotage. Today is the day to return that phone call, start an exercise regimen, or tackle a new project.

- **Choose to feel hopeful, not hopeless.** If you've experienced heartache due to life's disappointments (and who hasn't?), it's tempting to give up—or go through the motions even though your ambitions seem futile. Hopefulness, however, is an attitude that will sustain you through hard times.

- **Seek guidance from an objective source.** We often can't see our blind-spots because we are—obviously—blind to them. Many people engage in destructive behavior completely unaware they are doing so. Or they make unhealthy choices because no one has pointed them out. If you've experienced a failure that is setting you back, seek out a counselor, mentor, pastor, or trusted friend—someone who will speak truth into your life.

5. Shun Perfectionism

Perfectionists are people who expect themselves to always perform, well ... perfectly. They adopt an obsessive preoccupation with doing everything right. Since any mistake results in a negative response, perfectionists spend a great deal of time and energy trying to avoid doing anything wrong.

Perfectionism can operate in two ways—both extremely destructive. Like my client Chantel, you may find yourself going to any length to excel in whatever you do, spending great amounts of time and energy and shortchanging your own health and peace of mind to achieve at the highest level. You may become so focused on your performance that you lose sight of those around you, including family and friends.

On the opposite end of this frenetic activity, your perfectionism may lead you into a state of paralysis—which often, ironically, leads to experiences of failure. Feeling intense pressure, you might avoid preparing for a presentation or working on an important report. You may start projects only to leave them lying around for weeks.

PERFECTIONISTS MAY BECOME SO FOCUSED ON PERFORMANCE THAT THEY LOSE SIGHT OF THOSE AROUND THEM, INCLUDING FAMILY AND FRIENDS.

As long as they are unfinished, you haven't actually failed. You can still visualize all the rewards of success without suffering any of the negative consequences of failure. Your life becomes a series of projects that you have never started or that you have started but never completed.

STEPS TO OVERCOME PERFECTIONISM

If you are a perfectionist and tired of trying to reach impossible standards, start with these seven steps to become more balanced.

1. **Identify underlying beliefs that drive your need for perfection.** Maybe you grew up with impossible-to-please parents, or with overachieving siblings, or as part of a strict religious community. Often just realizing the roots of your perfectionism will jump-start the process of overcoming it.

2. **Accept imperfections in others.** Practicing compassion for other people is good training for learning to show compassion for yourself.

3. **Retrain your brain.** Perfectionists have become conditioned to think in terms of black or white, good or bad, all or nothing. If you've learned unhealthy mental patterns, you can also learn new and healthy ones.

4. **Listen to your thoughts.** Beware of those automatic thoughts that shout, *You're not good enough! You're going to blow it!* Identifying those thoughts is a step toward countering them with more reasonable ones.

5. **Receive compliments.** If your boss, a coworker, or a friend offers a sincere compliment, resist the urge to minimize or deflect: "Thanks, but...." A simple thank-you—without the "but"—will do just fine.

6. **Strive for excellence, not perfection.** Excellence means doing your best and holding yourself to high standards while realizing that perfection is unattainable. Matthew 5:48 says, "Be perfect ... as your heavenly Father is perfect"; but here the word *perfect* means "to be complete, mature, grown up in one's likeness to God's benevolence."[17] Instead of doing everything perfectly every time, think in terms of progress and perseverance in growing to be more like Jesus—even after myriad failures.

7. **Recognize your self-worth.** Most people tie their sense of value to performance and accomplishments. You'll gain freedom if you can learn to accept that real worth is based on inner qualities.

6. Banish *the* Inner Critic

Perhaps you live at the opposite end of the spectrum and are painfully aware of your "innumerable" flaws already. That's because barely a minute goes by when you aren't reminded of them by a relentless critic—your own thoughts. It's as if a two-bit judge has set up court in your mind, handing out harsh verdicts left and right. Do any of the following scenarios sound familiar?

- You received a mediocre annual review from your boss. ***Inner Critic:*** *You stink at this kind of work and should give up!*

- You offended someone by a comment you made on social media. ***Inner Critic:*** *You're an insensitive jerk with no social skills!*

- You applied for a loan and discovered that your credit score is in the "poor" category. ***Inner Critic:*** *You've always been lousy at finances and always will be.*

- You got a D on the final exam. ***Inner Critic:*** *Further proof that you're a loser!*

- Your teenager ended up in rehab. ***Inner Critic:*** *You've always been a sorry excuse for a parent.*

The point is, we take a lot of abuse inside our own heads, far more than we ever would from someone following us around shouting insults. Most people learn to tune it out or at least take it with a grain of salt. But some people actually agree with this daily torrent of negative judgment. It's easy to see how this can lead to a mental inferno of self-loathing and anger that sets fire to everything it touches.

ANYTIME YOUR HEART CONDEMNS YOU, ANSWER IT WITH THE TRUTH ABOUT HOW GOD VIEWS YOU.

Freedom lies in asking yourself, *Is this the way God sees me? Are these the labels he would attach to me: loser, failure, sorry excuse for a parent?* The answer is obvious: Never! His thoughts of us always rise out of his unfathomable love. The proof is in his sacrifice for our sake: "This is how we know what love is: Jesus Christ laid down his life for us.... If our hearts condemn us, we know that God is greater than our hearts, and he knows everything" (1 John 3:16, 20).

Anytime your heart condemns you, answer it with the truth about how God views you. In the light of his Word, hateful self-anger won't last long.

7. Recognize False Guilt

For many people, experiences of failure bring on feelings of guilt, which may or may not be justified.

Suppose you volunteer to spearhead a fundraising event for your child's school. You decide to hold a carnival with food, games, and entertainment. But because you have never taken on a big endeavor like this before, a few important details fall through the cracks: Publicity isn't robust enough to attract large numbers of people. Some parents who volunteered to set up game booths cancel at the last minute, and backups haven't been secured. To top it all off, the folks selling food and drinks have their own issues, running out of supplies and leaving carnival-goers hungry and thirsty.

WHENEVER YOU MAKE A MISTAKE, ASK YOURSELF, *DID THIS HAPPEN BECAUSE I AM SIMPLY AN IMPERFECT HUMAN BEING, OR DID I ACTUALLY FAIL?*

Afterward, you have to admit the event was a dud. Lots of complaints and very little fundraising. You tell yourself, "I totally blew it! It's all my fault!" You feel guilty for disappointing everyone at the school. But eventually you realize it was a matter of poor planning and bad luck. The carnival wasn't truly a failure but a worthy effort that produced lackluster results—and something you will learn from. You're able to recognize false guilt and reframe it within the truth of the matter.

On the other hand, feelings of guilt can sometimes be justified. Let's say that last Friday night you went out with your friends, drank too much alcohol, and got a DUI on the way home. Afterward you would probably feel guilty (as well as hung over). That guilt is appropriate and justified because you used very poor judgment that seriously endangered yourself and others.

You see what I'm saying? Feelings of shame that are prompted by making a mistake—by being human—can weigh us down and hold us back. But they don't need to. And they shouldn't.

Conversely, justified feelings of guilt can and should instruct us and motivate us to make changes in our lives. Guilt can teach us valuable lessons in the way we should improve our behavior and decision-making.

Whenever you make a mistake, ask yourself, *Did this happen because I am simply an imperfect human being, or did I actually fail?* If it's the former, grant yourself grace and patience; if it's the latter, seek to do everything you can to avoid similar situations in the future.

8. Tame Your Toxic Emotions

The humiliation of failure can make you want to hide in a deep, dark cave until the end of time. Attempting to suppress these natural reactions when you're experiencing a big setback is guaranteed to make matters worse. But at the same time, it takes discernment and discipline to recognize that serving as a long-term host of unhealthy emotions such as shame will only pull you deeper into despair instead of propelling you forward. Here are a few reasons to move on.

- **Toxic emotions blind you to opportunity.** An old proverb says, "Trouble always arrives at your door with a gift in its hands." But there's a catch—you must reach out and take it. Sometimes the gift-wrapping on such opportunity looks more like camouflage, because white-hot pain, anger, and grief are bullies that dominate and intimidate every other thought. Much depends on your ability to see the possibilities in your misfortune, and taming your toxic emotions is the place to start.

- **Toxic emotions build up.** Modern research suggests that our thoughts and feelings are far more than insubstantial shadows. They leave a distinct footprint in the body. In essence, your unbridled emotions are homemade drugs that exert a powerful effect. What starts out as healthy grief may morph into deep depression—or travel the other direction toward crippling rage. It is wise to deal with your feelings long before they have a chance to gang up on you.

■ **Toxic emotions lead to toxic behavior.** It would be bad enough if runaway feelings only affected your inner world. But the truth is, left unchecked, they will poison your actions as well, motivating choices that are unhealthy and unhelpful, potentially alienating the very friends you need to put your life back together. Or your emotions could drive you to shut down and withdraw completely, or to flirt with damaging addictions just to find relief. There are innumerable ways to face your feelings and drain them of unhealthy potential—meditation, exercise, prayer, therapy, and other healing activities that get you "out of your head" and ready for what comes next. Finding the ones that work for you will help you bounce back from failure.

9. Refuse *to* Give Up

To help you press on through difficult times, make the commitment to never quit pursuing the worthy goal of becoming the person God created you to be. Your ability to withstand the storms of your life will depend on your choice to never give up, no matter what challenges and failures come your way. Reigniting your passion for life requires that you have courage even when you are afraid, and that you act with boldness even when you feel lost and defeated.

YOUR ABILITY TO WITHSTAND THE STORMS OF YOUR LIFE WILL DEPEND ON YOUR CHOICE TO NEVER GIVE UP.

Moving beyond your greatest fears and feelings of failure allows God to give you the power to make good decisions and find deep-down peace. And as you regain your life, rebuild your self-esteem, and recover from setbacks, you will find strength to keep growing.

Regardless of how others might misunderstand you, you *can* keep going. When they cannot understand the pain and circumstances involved in your failure, you do not need to give up. And even if they are unwilling to forgive your mistakes, you can still speak the truth honestly and move past their rejection with a peaceful heart.

PRESS ON TOWARD THE GOAL

The apostle Paul wrote, "One thing I do: Forgetting what is behind and straining toward what is ahead, I press on toward the goal to win the prize for which God has called me heavenward in Christ Jesus" (Philippians 3:13–14).

- What is the one goal you are pressing toward?

  _____

  _____

- When you feel like giving up, what keeps you moving forward?

  _____

  _____

- Despite the failures you've experienced, what is one thing you can do today to move in a positive direction?

  _____

  _____

10. Focus *on* Today

Feelings of failure often negatively shift our perspective about the past, present, and future. Therefore, it is helpful to go back to the basics of affirming the promise and potential of *this* day—not fretting about what tomorrow may bring.

A good way to incorporate this practice of today-focus is by reading or reciting at least one particular verse of the Lord's Prayer: "Give us today our daily bread" (Matthew 6:11). The key words *today* and *daily* teach us that this moment in time is all we really need to focus on.

I'm pretty sure if human beings had written the portion of the Lord's Prayer that asks for provision, it might go something like this:

> *"Give us this day* ... our monthly expenses."

> *"Give us this day* ... a comfortable annual income."

> *"Give us this day* ... a secure and ample nest egg for retirement."

Praying for "daily bread"—for only what we need to live on—isn't an idea we would come up with on our own. You might have heard the old saying, "Enough is as good as a feast." But the truth is that few of us really believe it. Today's feast never quite satisfies our hunger to know, "Will there be enough tomorrow? What if ...?"

There are an infinite number of ways to complete that sentence. Life is full of potentially painful outcomes that can lead to the haunting fear of poverty, lack, and abandonment. Against this relentless tide of uncertainty, we build fragile levies out of anything we can stockpile. "Surplus" and "security" have come to mean the same thing, but we all know that in the whole world there isn't enough material wealth to cover all the possible "What ifs." And this certainly contributes to our fear of future failures and our perspective of failures already experienced.

Fortunately, God has an alternate plan. Unlike earthly strategies, his way is immune to every misfortune and disaster. He offers us the only true source of security: *a relationship with himself.*

Don't misunderstand. God doesn't wave a magic wand and make uncertainty disappear. Instead, every new and frightening "What if" has a single solution: Faith in God's promise to care for you—today. It isn't necessary to know where his provision is stored or how it will reach you tomorrow. The secret to real security lies in simply knowing God and choosing to take him at his Word. That's an investment that always pays a dividend—and helps keep our failures in proper perspective. After all, what could be more secure than living by faith each day, trusting in the care of the living God?

FOR REFLECTION

■ Make a list of the things you truly need today. At the end of the day, reflect on whether God provided what was on your list.

_____

_____

■ Your feelings about past failures are real and shouldn't be avoided. Still, it's healthy to reflect on the gifts and blessings you enjoyed today. What are some that helped you take a tiny step beyond your painful feelings?

_____

_____

■ Read Matthew 6:25–34 aloud. Personalize the passage by inserting troublesome needs from your own life when Jesus says, "Do not worry about ..."

_____

_____

11. Rejoice Rather *than* Resent

I know it sounds ridiculous to "rejoice" when experiencing the aftermath of failure. Our natural inclination is to do just the opposite: fret, fume, and fuss. But in my many years of working with people who have failed in various ways, I've come to firmly believe that we all have a secret weapon that's often overlooked and infrequently utilized: gratitude.

WHEN WE SEIZE THE OPPORTUNITY TO EXPRESS GRATITUDE, WE SEIZE A WEAPON THAT WILL HELP US PREVAIL OVER RESENTMENT AND DISAPPOINTMENT.

Practicing thankfulness is a tool that empowers us to move on after failure. Here's why: When we're hurting, our thoughts and emotions are drawn to the source of pain like iron chips to a magnet. We dwell on our weaknesses, our poor decisions, and our disappointments. Choosing to be thankful, however, draws our

thoughts and emotions away from our distress and places them on God and his blessings. Simply put, gratitude dramatically shifts our focus.

This doesn't mean we deny the pain that exists. It doesn't mean we adopt a phony attitude of sunshine and sweetness. But as we look lucidly at bad things that have happened, we can also give thanks for all the good.

We can choose to be gloomy and angry—or grateful and appreciative. We can either say "I will resent" or "I will rejoice." Our decision makes all the difference between experiencing the freedom to move forward and remaining bound up by bitterness.

The apostle Paul encouraged us to "rejoice always, pray continually, give thanks in all circumstances" (1 Thessalonians 5:16–18). This means to give thanks not just when things are going well. When we seize the opportunity to express gratitude, we seize a weapon that will help us prevail over resentment and disappointment.

EXPRESSING GRATITUDE

■ In your own words, explain how gratitude serves the process of overcoming failure.

_____

_____

■ It goes without saying that no one wants to experience failure. But can you identify one or two blessings that have come from a difficult situation in the past or present?

_____

_____

■ In the space below or in your journal, make a list of all the things you're thankful for—big (good health, a supportive family) or small (birds chirping, a hot bath). In the days ahead, continue to add to it, and thank God, the giver of all that's good, for every big and small blessing.

_____

_____

_____

12. Dream Big, *but* Live Now

Antonio was a talented singer and songwriter. In high school, he won second place in a national songwriting contest. He had a small following of loyal fans in the local music scene. Everyone agreed that Antonio had great potential.

He was also miserable. Antonio's life was a frantic race to hit it big. He spent long hours cultivating contacts and promoting his music. Every dime he earned went into workshops and demo recordings. He barely had time to eat.

Two days before his thirtieth birthday, Antonio collapsed from exhaustion during a performance. I met him when his family insisted he seek counseling. "I'll sleep when I'm dead," he told me the first time I met him. "I'm so close to my big break—I can't stop now."

On one hand, Antonio's work ethic was admirable. He was not afraid to roll up his sleeves and doggedly pursue his goal. But on the other hand, he clearly confused what he hoped to do in his life with who he was. In the absence of overt "success," he considered himself a failure. His dream was holding him hostage until the future he imagined arrived. In the meantime, his health and happiness took a nosedive.

When you build your identity around something you hope for, you'll live in the limbo of "If … then": "If I get this promotion, then I'll be secure." "If we can afford a new house, then I'll be satisfied." Present-moment awareness is the key to escaping this destructive cycle. It opens a gap between the real you and your imaginary future "identity." Here and now, you understand you are larger than anything you think, feel, or do.

FULLY ACCEPT WHO AND WHERE YOU ARE RIGHT NOW … EVEN AS YOU ENDEAVOR TO GROW AND DEVELOP.

I'm all for maximizing potential and striving for high goals. I'm not at all in favor of doing these things at the expense of joy and happiness today. Your fulfillment in life need not be wrapped up in your potential for success. Fully accept who and where you are right now … even as you endeavor to grow and develop.

13. Do Your Best

We don't have control over most variables in our lives, and that's a big reason why it makes no sense to tie our sense of value to them. One variable we do have control over is the commitment to do our best. This may involve our planning, creativity, diligence, perseverance, and wise use of resources. If we hitch our self-worth to factors like these, we will probably end up feeling good about ourselves and keeping our mistakes in a balanced perspective.

The apostle Paul speaks to this directly: "Pay careful attention to your own work, for then you will get the satisfaction of a job well done, and you won't need to compare yourself with anyone else" (Galatians 6:4 NLT).

14. Dare *to* Not Compare

Speaking of comparison, feelings of failure are compounded tenfold when we measure our own achievements against those of others. When we hold ourselves to the standards of someone we consider a "winner," we are sure to come away feeling like a "loser." This is nonsense.

Sadly, the society we live in teaches us to treat each other as competitors, and we feel much better about ourselves if we prove to be more successful than someone else. We compare our looks, physiques, intelligence levels, incomes, careers, athletic abilities, social standings, houses, and cars. As if comparing ourselves isn't problematic enough, many parents compare their children to other kids. Who is smarter, cuter, funnier, more athletic, more polite, more obedient, more spiritual, more artistic, more musical?

I could go on and on, but if you are a person who compares, you know there is no end to this kind of compulsion. The temptation to compare yourself to others in an effort to demonstrate your worth and importance is a dead-end process—not only because you so frequently find yourself "less than," but also because it never works. It doesn't matter if you make a hundred different comparisons and find yourself to be better at each one than someone else. You still will not believe you are valuable and worthwhile if you didn't think so before you began comparing.

But that's not the only tragic consequence of this highly popular interpersonal pursuit. Another damaging result is that it sets us against one another. How could I possibly cheer like crazy when you make progress in your life if your success threatens my own sense of well-being?

THE TEMPTATION TO COMPARE YOURSELF TO OTHERS IN AN EFFORT TO DEMONSTRATE YOUR WORTH AND IMPORTANCE IS A DEAD-END PROCESS.

The Bible tells us to "rejoice with those who rejoice; mourn with those who mourn" (Romans 12:15). How often we are tempted to twist that around by feeling better about ourselves when someone else's mistake seems worse than our own. Let's agree not to go there. In times of downfall, yours or mine, let's lift each other up.

■ ■ ■

I started this chapter with the account of my client Chantel, who had achieved incredible success in her professional life but, as she eventually discovered, was failing in her personal life. I'm so glad to say that after a hard look at her life priorities and inner world, she was able to learn from her failures and repair the damage done by choices she'd made. After months of therapy, Chantel and Marcus moved steadily toward mending their troubled marriage. And eventually they worked together to regain trust and connectedness with their children, who had become isolated and cynical amid their parents' struggles.

EVERY STORY— INCLUDING YOURS—COMES WITH THE OPPORTUNITY FOR REDEMPTION AND GIANT LEAPS FORWARD.

This isn't to say that every story has a happy ending. Failure does indeed come with consequences and pain. But every story— including yours—also comes with the opportunity for redemption and giant leaps forward.

A NEW PERSPECTIVE

Reframing Your Failure

❏ **I will resolve to move forward, not backward.**

"Forget the former things; do not dwell on the past. See, I am doing a new thing! Now it springs up; do you not perceive it? I am making a way in the wilderness and streams in the wasteland." (Isa. 43:18–19)

❏ **I will come clean about my mistakes.**

"Though your sins are like scarlet, they shall be as white as snow; though they are red as crimson, they shall be like wool." (Isa 1:18)

❏ **I will forgive myself.**

"Anyone who belongs to Christ has become a new person. The old life is gone; a new life has begun! And all of this is a gift from God, who brought us back to himself through Christ." (2 Cor. 5:17–18 NLT)

❏ **I will avoid self-sabotaging behavior.**

"Do you not know that your bodies are temples of the Holy Spirit, who is in you, whom you have received from God? You are not your own; you were bought at a price. Therefore honor God with your bodies." (1 Cor. 6:19-20)

❏ **I will shun perfectionism.**

"We all stumble in many ways. Anyone who is never at fault in what they say is perfect, able to keep their whole body in check." (James 3:2)

❏ **I will banish the inner critic.**

"Brothers and sisters, whatever is true, whatever is noble, whatever is right, whatever is pure, whatever is lovely, whatever is admirable—if anything is excellent or praiseworthy—think about such things." (Phil. 4:8)

❏ **I will recognize and reject false guilt.**

"This is how we know that we belong to the truth and how we set our hearts at rest in his presence: If our hearts condemn us, we know that God is greater than our hearts, and he knows everything. Dear friends, if our hearts do not condemn us, we have confidence before God and receive from him anything we ask, because we keep his commands and do what pleases him." (1 John 3:19–22)

❏ **I will tame my toxic emotions.**

"Whoever is slow to anger is better than the mighty, and he who rules his spirit than he who takes a city." (Proverbs 16:32 ESV)

❑ **I will refuse to give up.**

"One thing I do: Forgetting what is behind and straining toward what is ahead, I press on toward the goal to win the prize for which God has called me heavenward in Christ Jesus." (Phil. 3:13–14)

❑ **I will focus only on what I need today.**

"Give us today our daily bread." (Matt. 6:11)

❑ **I will choose to rejoice rather than resent.**

"Rejoice always, pray continually, give thanks in all circumstances; for this is God's will for you in Christ Jesus." (1 Thess. 5:16–18)

"Consider it pure joy, my brothers and sisters, whenever you face trials of many kinds, because you know that the testing of your faith produces perseverance." (James 1:2–3)

❑ **I will dream big, but live in the now.**

"Seek first his kingdom and his righteousness, and all these things will be given to you as well." (Matt. 6:33)

❏ **I will choose to do my best, despite my circumstances, recognizing it's the only factor I can control.**

"Pay careful attention to your own work, for then you will get the satisfaction of a job well done, and you won't need to compare yourself with anyone else" (Galatians 6:4 NLT)

❏ **I will dare to not compare myself with others.**

"A heart at peace gives life to the body, but envy rots the bones." (Prov. 14:30)

"Make it your ambition to lead a quiet life: You should mind your own business and work with your hands." (1 Thess. 4:11–12)

The Ultimate Antidote

What if you could accept your mistakes and failures without taking a big hit to your self-esteem and future hopes?

What if you could establish that you are valuable and treasured no matter what?

What if you knew that there is no need to establish your identity on the basis of your success and failures?

What if you were to look in the mirror each morning and think, *I like this person, despite the obvious shortcomings?*

You can experience all of this by accepting God's grace—his offer of unqualified, unreserved love. Consider this: "He has saved us and called us to a holy life—not because of anything we have done but because of his own purpose and grace. This grace was given us in Christ Jesus before the beginning of time, but it has now been revealed through the appearing of our Savior, Christ Jesus, who has destroyed death and has brought life and immortality to light through the gospel" (1 Timothy 1:9–10).

I feel extremely blessed to have grown up in a loving, God-honoring family and faith community. I am so grateful. Yet as I look back, I realize that the church we attended placed a big emphasis on *doing* rather than *being*. There was plenty of talk about "God's grace," but not much action or attitude to demonstrate what that truly meant.

WHEN WE PLACE OUR FAITH IN GOD, OUR VALUE AND WORTH ARE ESTABLISHED FOR ALL TIME.

When I discovered years later that unconditional love is the foundational truth of the Christian faith, I at first struggled to understand what this meant. I'd heard phrases such as *God's grace*, *unmerited favor*, and *sacrificial love*, but I had never experienced these ideas deep down. Nobody had clarified this unbelievably good news during my formative years.

As an adult, well into my training to become a psychologist, I came to understand that when we place our faith in God, our value and worth are established for all time. His love for us is total—and totally unconditional. No "success" will cause him to love us any more, and no "failure" will cause him to love us any less.

As you work through your feelings of failure, remember that your most powerful healing source comes from the pages of Scripture, from God's mouth to your ears. The apostle Paul wrote,

> *I am convinced that nothing can ever separate us from God's love. Neither death nor life, neither angels nor demons, neither our fears for today nor our worries about tomorrow—not even the powers of hell can separate us from God's love. No power in the sky above or in the earth below—indeed, nothing in all creation will ever be able to separate us from the love of God that is revealed in Christ Jesus our Lord.*

Romans 8:38–39 NLT

Understanding that you are freely and completely loved by God will keep your mistakes and failures in proper perspective. You do not need to win God's approval by being successful, and you will not lose his love by experiencing failures. You are accepted exactly as you are—the good, the bad, and the ugly.

If we were perfect people with perfect lives, we wouldn't need grace. Truth wouldn't be difficult to accept, for it wouldn't contain the wreckage of unwise choices and poor judgment. In order to accept ourselves and others in a flawed world, however, grace is imperative.

- Grace allows damaged relationships to heal.

- Grace untangles the knots of bitterness and blame.

- Grace empowers us to keep our mistakes in proper perspective.

- Grace removes the weight of guilt and shame from our heart and soul.

And all of this leads us to the most important point in the entire book: *Failure is never final, because God's love for you is forever.* Rest well in that promise!

"GOD SO LOVED THE WORLD THAT HE GAVE HIS ONE AND ONLY SON, THAT WHOEVER BELIEVES IN HIM SHALL NOT PERISH BUT HAVE ETERNAL LIFE."

—John 3:16

GIVE YOURSELF GRACE

Think of a situation in your life that caused you regret. Now envision yourself during that time—it might have been long ago or recently. Tell yourself the truth of the matter, fully and completely—acknowledge that you have disappointed yourself and others, but also affirm that you are worthy of love and acceptance. Offer yourself forgiveness and grace by agreeing that you have learned from the situation and are ready to move forward as a wiser person.

Notes

1   Diane K. Osbon, ed., *A Joseph Campbell Companion: Reflections on the Art of Living* (New York: HarperPerennial, 1991), 24.

2   Robert Bly, *Iron John: A Book about Men* (New York: Vintage Books, 1992), 71.

3   Neal Gabler, *Walt Disney: The Triumph of the American Imagination* (New York: Vintage Books, 2007), 43–77.

4   Eudie Pak, "Walt Disney's Rocky Road to Success," last updated June 17, 2020. *Biography*. https://www.biography.com/news/walt-disney-failures (June 28, 2022).

5   "Lincoln's Failures?" *Abraham Lincoln Online: Education Links*. http://www.abrahamlincolnonline.org/lincoln/education/failures.htm (June 29, 2022).

6   Mayo Oshin, "J. K. Rowling on How to Deal with Failure in Life and Work," January 17, 2019. *MayoOshin.com*. https://www.mayooshin.com/j-k-rowling-how-to-deal-with-failure-in-life/.

7   "Steve Jobs." *AppleInsider.com*. https://appleinsider.com/inside/steve-jobs (June 29, 2022).

8 Janet B. Pascal, *Who Was Dr. Seuss?* (New York: Penguin Workshop, 2011), 16–17.

9 Ronald de Leeuw, ed., *The Letters of Vincent van Gogh*, trans. Arnold Pomerans (London: Penguin Books, 1996), 469.

10 Winston Churchill, quoted in "Success: What Churchill Really Said," May 6, 2019. *Richard M. Langworth. https:// richardlangworth.com/success* (June 30, 3022).

11 "Famous Quotes by Vince Lombardi." *Vince Lombardi [official site]. http://www.vincelombardi.com/quotes.html* (July 5, 2022).

12 "80th Anniversary of Harrow School Speech," September 30, 2021. *International Churchill Society. https://winstonchurchill .org/publications/churchill-bulletin/bulletin-160-oct-2021/ never-give-in-4/* (July 5, 2022).

13 "Thomas Edison," last edited May 22, 2022. *Wikiquote (https://en.wikiquote.org/wiki/Thomas_Edison)*, as quoted in *The Edison & Ford Quote Book* (2003), ed. Edison & Ford Winter Estates.

14 *Merriam-Webster's Collegiate Dictionary*, 10th ed. (1993), s.v. "shame."

15 Attributed to Robert Green Ingersoll.

16 Quoted in Frank Lewis Dyer and Thomas Commerford Martin, *Edison: His Life and Inventions, vol. 2* (New York: Harper & Brothers, 1910), 616.

17 Philip W. Comfort, ed., *Cornerstone Biblical Commentary: The Gospel of Matthew; The Gospel of Mark*, vol. 11 (Carol Stream, IL: Tyndale House, 2006), 95.

Image Credits

Images used under license from Shutterstock.com: STUDIO DREAM, cover and pp. 3, 5, 11, 15, 19, 31, 37, 45, 55, 61, 63, 77, 85, 88, 91, 99, 101, 103, 109; CHUYKO SERGEY p. 7; siam.pukkato p. 8; maxsattana p. 9; Antonio Guillem pp. 12, 25; Ground Picture p. 16; Tom Saga p. 17; Russian Huzau p. 18; Tiko Aramyan p. 21; Kleber Cordeiro p. 27; Dinj fizkes pp. 46, 89; Friends Stock p. 48; KieferPix p. 49; Carlos Amarillo p. 50; peamathz2812 p. 52; ImageFlow p. 53; Deer worawut p. 56; Creativa Images p. 64; HAKINMHAN p. 66; Ariya J p. 67; patpitchaya p. 68; Evgeniia Primavera p. 70; Take Photo p. 71; izf p. 72; Kaspars Grinvalds p. 75; Wirestock Creators p. 79; Krakenimages.com p. 80; chaiyapruek younprasert p. 84; mvc_stock p. 90; eamesBot p. 93; Thx4Stock p. 94; Randy Hume p. 96; Juice Flair p. 97; Love You Stock p. 104; Pazargic Liviu p. 107